PYTHON DATA SCIENCE

The Practical Beginner's Guide to Learn Python Data Science in One Day Step-By-Step (#2020 updated version | Effective Computer Programming)

Steve Tudor

Text   **Copyright**   ©

All rights reserved. No part of this guide may be reproduced in any form without permission in writing from the publisher except in the case of brief quotations embodied in critical articles or reviews.

Legal & Disclaimer

The information contained in this book and its contents is not designed to replace or take the place of any form of medical or professional advice; and is not meant to replace the need for independent medical, financial, legal or other professional advice or services, as may be required. The content and information in this book has been provided for educational and entertainment purposes only.

The content and information contained in this book has been compiled from sources deemed reliable, and it is accurate to the best of the Author's knowledge, information and belief. However, the Author cannot guarantee its accuracy and validity and cannot be held liable for any errors and/or omissions. Further, changes are periodically made to this book as and when needed. Where appropriate and/or necessary, you must consult a professional (including but not limited to your doctor, attorney, financial advisor or such other professional advisor) before using any of the suggested remedies, techniques, or information in this book.

Upon using the contents and information contained in this book, you agree to hold harmless the Author from and against any damages, costs, and expenses, including any legal fees potentially resulting from the application of any of the information provided by this book. This disclaimer applies to any loss, damages or injury caused by the use and application, whether directly or indirectly, of any advice or information presented, whether for breach of contract, tort, negligence, personal injury, criminal intent, or under any other cause of action.

You agree to accept all risks of using the information presented inside this book.

You agree that by continuing to read this book, where appropriate and/or necessary, you shall consult a professional (including but not limited to your doctor, attorney, or financial advisor or such other advisor as needed) before using any of the suggested remedies, techniques, or information in this book.

Table of Contents

Introduction 7

Part 1 : FUNDAMENTALS OF DATA SCIENCE 9

Chapter 1. what is data science 10

Chapter 2. different areas of application 13

Chapter 3. history of data science 15

Chapter 4. data science and artificial intelligence 18

Chapter 5. data science tips and tricks 22

Part 2: DATA SCIENCE WITH PYTHON 29

Chapter 6. Introduction to NumPy 30

Chapter 7. packages installations 34

Chapter 8. manipulating array 46

Chapter 9. conditional selection, ... 49

Chapter 10. NumPy Array Operations, ... 53

Chapter 11. Pandas, ... 55

Chapter 12. Data frames, ... 60

Chapter 13. Missing Data, ... 70

Chapter 14. Group-By 75

Chapter 15. Reading and writing data 78

    Read 78

CSV (comma separated variables) & Excel 78

   Write 79

   Html 80

Part 3: MACHINE LEARNING WITH PYTHON 84

Chapter 15. What is machine learning 85

Chapter 16. categories of machine learning 86

   Supervised Learning 86

   Unsupervised Learning 86

   Reinforcement Learning 87

Chapter 17. qualitative examples of machine learning applications 88

Chapter 18. python and machine learning 92

Chapter 19. machine learning and data science, ... 95

Chapter 20. model validation 96

Chapter 21. machine learning case studies 98

   Where Do You Come From, Where Do You Go, Deep Learning? .101

Part 4 : WORKBOOK 104

   Matplotlib 105

   Interactive Visualization 106

      Quiz 107

      Answers 108

Conclusion 110

Introduction

There are different tools that can be used for data analysis. Examples of these include **SAS** programming, **Hadoop**, **R** programming, **SQL**, **Python**, and others. Amongst these tools, Python has a very unique feature as it is a general feature programming language whose syntax is easy to grasp.

Python has been in existence for a long time and it has been used in many industries like oil, scientific computing, gas, physics, finance, signal processing, and many others. It has been used for the development of applications like **YouTube** and it has played a great role in powering the internal infrastructure of **Google**.

Python is a powerful tool for data science due to its flexibility and being open source. It is well known for its many libraries that can be used for data manipulation Examples of such libraries include **Pandas**, **Scikit-Learn**, **TensorFlow**, **PyTorch**, **NumPy**, **Scipy**, and **PyBrain**. Alongside these, there is the **Cython library** that helps in converting Python code to run in a C environment to reduce runtime, **PyMySQL** that helps in connecting to **MySQL databases**, extracting data and executing queries.

Data analysis goes hand-in-hand with data visualization. Python has made a number of improvements to overtake its competitor, R, in data visualization. We now have APIs like **Plotly** and libraries like **Matplotlib**, **Pygal**, **ggplot**, **NetworkX**, and others for data visualization. Python can also be integrated with other data visualization tools like Tableau and **Qlikview** using **TabPy** and **win32com** respectively.

Currently, **Hadoop** is the largest platform for data analysis. Python is compatible with Hadoop, which has made it a widely adopted language for data analysis. The **PyDoop** API provides us with access to HDFS API to connect our program to the HDFS installation. After that, we can write, read and get information on directories, files as well as global file system properties. PyDoop also provides us with the *MapReduce API* to help us in solving complex problems with little programming.

Part 1 :

FUNDAMENTALS OF DATA SCIENCE

Chapter 1. what is data science

Data Science is an art. It is not a concept that one can teach a computer. Data analysts use different tools to achieve their tasks, right from linear regression to classification trees. Even though all these tools are known to the computer, it is the role of the data analyst to figure out a way in which he or she can gather all the tools and integrate them to data to

develop the correct answer to a question.

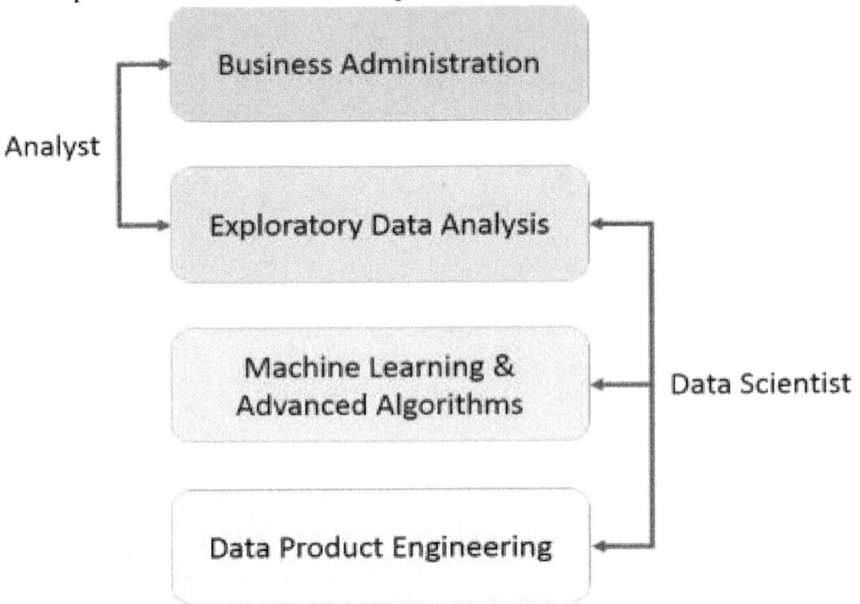

```
                  ┌──→ Business Administration
Analyst ──────────┤
                  └──→ Exploratory Data Analysis ←──┐
                                                    │
                       Machine Learning &      ←────┤ Data Scientist
                       Advanced Algorithms          │
                                                    │
                       Data Product Engineering ←───┘
```

The figure above shows that a Data Analyst explains whatever is happening by processing the history of the data. On the other hand, a A Data Scientist looks at the data from different perspectives and angles.

Therefore, Data Science helps an individual predict and make decisions by taking advantage of prescriptive analytics, machine learning, and predictive causal analytics.

- **Prescriptive Analytics.** If you need a model that has the intelligence and capability to make its own decisions, then prescriptive analytics is the best to use.

This new field delivers advice; it doesn't just predict, but it also recommends different prescribed actions and related outcomes. Data that is collected by the vehicle is used to train cars. You can further mine this data by using algorithms to reveal intelligence. This will allow your car to make decisions such as when to turn, which path to take, as well as when to speed up or slow down.

- **Machine Learning for Pattern Discovery.** Let's say that you don't have resources that you can apply to make predictions; it will require you to determine the hidden patterns in the data set to predict correctly. The most popular algorithm used in pattern discovery is Clustering. Assume that you work in a telephone company, and you want to determine a network by installing towers in the region. Therefore, you may use the clustering technique to determine the tower location that will make sure all users have the maximum signal strength.

- **Make Predictions with Machine Learning.** If you can predict the future trend of a company, then Machine Learning algorithms are the best to go with. This falls under supervised learning; it is called supervised because data is already present that you can use to train machines.

Data Science and Discovery of Data Insight

The main aspect of Data Science is to discover findings from data. It involves unearthing hidden insight that can allow companies to make smart business decisions. For example:

- **Highlighting key customer segments inside its base as well as special shopping behaviors in the segments. This directs messages to different market audiences.**
- **Netflix extracts data from movie viewing patterns to find out what drives user interest and uses it to make decisions.**

- **Proctor and Gamble make use of time series models to understand future demand. This allows a person to plan for production levels.**

But how do Data Scientists extract data insights? If you ever asked yourself this question, the answer is: it begins with data exploration. When faced with a difficult problem, Data Scientists become curious. They attempt to find leads and understand characteristics within the data. To achieve this, an individual must have a higher level of creativity.

Besides, they may choose to use quantitative techniques to move deeper. Some examples are time series forecasting, inferential models segmentation analysis, synthetic control experiments, and many more. The aim is to put together a forensic view of what the data means. Hence, data-driven insight is the key in delivering strategic guidance. In other words, the role of Data Scientists is to guide business stakeholders so that they can learn how to respond to findings.

Chapter 2. different areas of application

While there is a lot that you can do with data science, you must remember that it is mainly just a tool that you use in business. If you know how to use it properly and you make sure to stay efficient with it, data science can be a great tool that helps limit your risk and even make you more money. However, if you do not use it properly, it could easily cause a lot more harm to your business than it does good.

It is easy to become captivated with all of the possibilities that can come with data science. But if your business can't afford it or if you just try to use it without the right experience or knowledge, then you will end up costing your business a lot of money. Make sure that the data science team and the management team become are aware of some crucial points along the way.

What management needs to know

To get as much out of the wealth of data that a business has, and information on the Internet, management must think of the data analytically. If management is not able to do this, then they will become completely dependent on the results from data mining, and they won't think for themselves. There is a ton of information that comes from the data mining process, but you must think it through and combine your knowledge and expertise to get the best results.

Of course, this is not to say that the management needs to be data scientists to understand the information and to use it. It just means that the managers of an organization at least need to know some of the basics to appreciate the different opportunities that it will provide. You do not want to waste the valuable resources that data science can provide simply because you don't understand how it works or what all it can do for you and your company.

As a manager, there are a few things that you should be able to do, even if you are not a data scientist. You should be able to appreciate all the opportunities that this information provides, make sure that your data science team has the resources that it needs to get the job done and be willing to invest your time and money so that data experimentation occurs. Finally, you must be able to work with your team to ensure that they stay on track and help you get information to help move the business forward.

How data science gives a competitive advantage

Data science, as long as it is used correctly, can give a business a big competitive edge in their market. To have an advantage over the competition, you must make sure that you are always one to two steps ahead of them. This can be done through a willingness and the act of investing in new data assets and also the development of new capabilities and techniques. It also requires that you not only treat the investment and the results from this as an asset, but you must also treat your data science team and the field of data science in the same way.

With the best data science team, you will be able to gain the useful insights that you need to help move your business into the future. There are so many businesses that will just rely on experience and knowledge to help them. And if you have been in the industry for a long time, you will probably do well. Most of those who are new to an industry will end up failing with this though.

However, even if you are doing well, data science could provide you with some useful information and open up new doors that you may not have thought about in the past.

Chapter 3. history of data science

The history of deep learning can be traced back to 1943, when Warren McCulloch and Walter Pitts published a paper with a concept of Artificial Neuron(AN) to mimic the thought process. This Artificial neuron was based on the characteristic of a biological neuron of either being fully active to a stimulation or none at all. This behavior of biological neurons was observed in microelectrode readings from brain.

In 1957, Frank and Rosenblatt presented Mark I Perceptron Machine as the first implementation of the perceptron algorithm. The idea was to resemble the working of biological neurons to create an agent that can learn. This perceptron was a supervised binary linear classifier with adjustable weights. This functionality was implemented through following function:

Where, w is weights vector, X is inputs and b is bias.

For each input and output pair, this formula provided classification results. If the result/prediction did not match with output, the weight vector was updated through :

Where, is predicted/output of function, is actual output, is input vector and is weight vector.

It should be noted that back at that time, they implemented this functionality through a hardware machine with wires and connections (as shown in the figure below).

In 1960, Widrow and Hoff stacked these perceptrons and built a 3-layered (input layer, hidden layer, output layer), fully connected, feed-forward architecture for classification as a hardware implementation, called ADALINE. The architecture presented in the paper is shown in image below.

In 1960, Henry J. Kelley introduced a continuous back propagation model, which is currently used in learning weights of the model. In 1962, a simpler version of backpropagation based on chain rule was introduced by Stuart Dreyfus but these methods were inefficient. The backpropagation currently used in models was actually presented in 1980s.

In 1979, Fukushima designed a multi-layered convolutional neural network architecture, called Neocognitron, that could learn to recognize patterns in images. The network resembled to current day architectures but wasn't exactly the same. It also allowed to manually adjust the weight of certain connections. Many concepts from Neocognitron continue to be used. The layered connections in perceptrons allowed to develop a variety of neural networks. For several patterns present in the data, Selective Attention Model could distinguish and separate them.

In 1970, Seppo Linnainmaa presented automatic differentiation to efficiently compute the derivative of a differentiable composite function using chain rule. Its application, later in 1986, led to the backpropagation of errors in multilayer perceptrons. This was when Geoff Hinton, Williams and Rumelhart presented a paper to demonstrate that backpropagation in neural networks provides interesting distribution representations. In 1989, Yann LeCun, currently, Director of AI Research Facebook, provided first practical demonstration of backpropagation in convolutional neural networks to read handwritten digits at Bell Labs. Even though with backpropagation, deep neural networks were not being able to train well.

In 1995, Vapnik and Cortes introduced support vector machines for regression and classification of data. In 1997, Schmidhuber and Hochreiter introduced Long Short Term Memory (LSTM) for recurrent neural networks.

In all these years, a major hindering constraint was computed but in 1999, computers started to become faster at processing data and Graphical Processing Units (GPUs) were introduced. This immensely increased the compute power.

In 2006, Hinton and Salakhutdinov presented a paper that reinvigorated research in deep learning. This was the first time when a proper 10 layer convolutional neural network was trained properly. Instead of training 10 layers using backpropagation, they came up with an unsupervised pre-training scheme, called Restricted Boltzmann Machine. This was a 2 step approach for training. In the first step, each layer of the network was trained using unsupervised objective. In the second step, all the layers were stacked together for backpropagation.

Later in 2009, Fei-Fei Li, a professor at Stanford university launched ImageNet, a large visual database designed for visual object recognition research containing more than 14 million hand-annotated images of 20,000 different object categories. This gave neural networks a huge edge as data of this order made it possible to train neural networks and achieve good results.

In 2010, neural networks got a lot of attention from the research community when Microsoft presented a paper on speech recognition and neural networks performed really well compared to other machine learning tools like SVMs and kernels. Specifically, they introduced neural network as a part of GMM and HMM framework and achieved huge improvements.

In 2012, a paper by Krizhevsky, Sutskever and Hinton showed that huge improvements are achieved through deep learning in the visual recognition domain. Their model, AlexNet outperformed all the other traditional computer vision methods in visual recognition task and won several international competitions. Since then, the field has exploded and several network architectures and ideas have been introduced like GANs.

Chapter 4. data science and artificial intelligence

Machine Learning will study an algorithm and let machines recognize patterns, develop models, and generate videos and images via learning. Machine Learning algorithms can be created using different methods such as clustering, decision trees, linear regression, and many more.

What is an Artificial Neural Network?

Artificial Neural Network is propelled by biological models of brain and biological neural networks. In brief, Artificial Neural Network (ANN) refers to a computational representation of the human neural network which alters human intelligence, memory, and reasoning. But why should the human brain system develop effective ML algorithms?

The major principle behind ANN is that neural networks are effective in advanced computations and hierarchical representation of knowledge. Dendrites and axons connect neurons into complex neural networks that can pass and exchange information as well as store intermediary computation results.

Therefore, a computational model of such systems can be effective in learning processes that resemble biological ones.

The perception algorithm created in 1957 was the trial to build a computational model of a biological neural network. However, advanced neural networks that have multiple layers, neurons, and nodes became possible just recently.

ANN is the reason for the recent success in computer vision and image recognition. Natural Language Processing and other applications of machine language seek to extract complex patterns from data. Neural networks are very useful when one wants to study nonlinear hypothesis that has many features. Building a precise hypothesis for a massive feature space may need one to have multiple high order polynomials that would inevitably result in overfitting. This is a situation where a model reveals random noise in data instead of the underlying patterns of relationships. The issue with overfitting involves image recognition problems. Here, each pixel represents a feature.

A Simple Neural Network That Has a Single Neuron

The simplest neural network has a single 'neuron' as shown below.

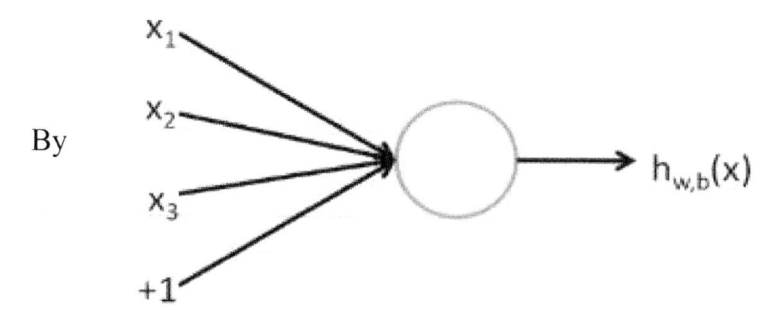

By

x_1, x_2, x_3, +1 → $h_{w,b}(x)$

applying a biological analogy, this neuron represents a computational unit that assumes inputs through electrical inputs and transfers them using axons to the next network output.

In the above simple neural network, dendrites refer to input features (x1, X2) and the output is the result of the hypothesis hw,b(x). Apart from the input features, the input layer of the neural network contains a bias unit that is equivalent to 1. A bias unit is required to apply a constant term in the function hypothesis.

In machine learning, the above network contains a single input layer, a hidden layer, and one output layer. To implement the learning process for this network, the input layer accepts input features for every training sample and feeds it to the activation function which computes the hypothesis in the hidden layer.

An activation function is a logistic regression applied in classification. However, other options are also possible. In the above case, a single neuron is similar to the input-output mapping defined by a logistic regression.

$$y = \varsigma(x) = \frac{1}{1+e^{-x}}$$

Multi-layered Neural Network

To understand how neural network operates, it is important to formalize the model and explain it in a real-world scenario. The image below represents a multilayer network that has three layers and various neurons. In this case, just like a single-neuron network, there is one input layer that has three inputs (x1, x2, x3) that has an added bias unit (+1). The second network layer is a hidden layer that has three units represented by activation functions. This is called a hidden layer because the values that are computed in it aren't observed. Basically, a neural network contains multiple hidden layers that pass advanced computations and functions from surface layers to the bottom of the neural network. The design of a neural network that has a lot of hidden layers is constantly used in Deep Learning.

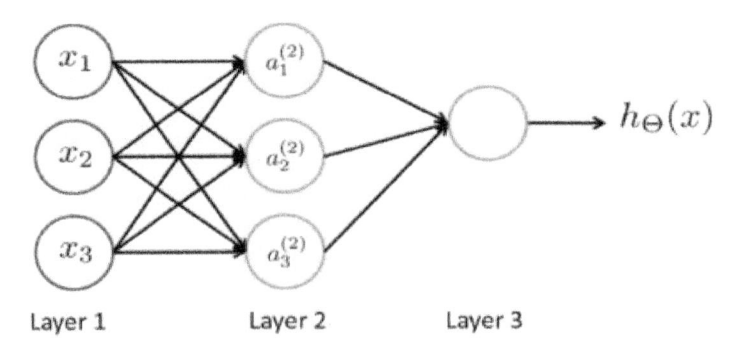

The hidden layer 2 has three neurons (a12, a22, a32). Each neuron of a hidden layer activates layer j. In this case, a unit a1 activates the first neuron of the second layer. Activation means that the value that is computed by function activation in this layer is output by the same node to the next layer.

Layer 3 is the output layer that receives results from the hidden layer and applies its own activation function. This layer calculates the final value of the hypothesis. Next, the cycle continues until that point when the neural network comes up with the model and weights which best predict the values of the training data.

Chapter 5. data science tips and tricks

One of the major strengths of Data Scientists is a strong background in Math and Statistics. Mathematics helps them create complex analytics. Besides this, they also use mathematics to create Machine Learning models and Artificial Intelligence. Similar to software engineering, Data Scientists must interact with the business side. This involves mastering the domain so that they can draw insights. Data Scientists need to analyze data to help a business, and this calls for some business acumen. Lastly, the results need to be assigned to the business in a way that anyone can understand. This calls for the ability to verbally and visually communicate advanced results and observations in a manner that a business can understand as well as work on it.

Therefore, it is important for any wannabe Data Scientists to have knowledge about Data Mining. Data Mining describes the process where raw data is structured in such a way where one can recognize patterns in the data via mathematical and computational algorithms.

Below are five mining techniques that every data scientist should know:

   1. **MapReduce**

The modern Data Mining applications need to manage vast amounts of data rapidly. To deal with these applications, one must use a new software stack. Since programming systems can retrieve parallelism from a computing cluster, a software stack has a new file system called a distributed file system.

The system has a larger unit than the disk blocks found in the normal operating system. A distributed file system replicates data to enforce security against media failures.

In addition to such file systems, a higher-level programming system has also been created. This is referred to as MapReduce. It is a form of computing which has been implemented in different systems such as Hadoop and Google's implementation. You can adopt a MapReduce implementation to control large-scale computations such that it can deal with hardware faults. You only need to write three functions. That is **Map** and **Reduce**, and then you can allow the system to control parallel execution and task collaboration.

2. Distance Measures

The major problem with Data Mining is reviewing data for similar items. An example can be searching for a collection of web pages and discovering duplicate pages. Some of these pages could be plagiarism or pages that have almost identical content but different in content. Other examples can include customers who buy similar products or discover images with similar characteristics.

Distance measure basically refers to a technique that handles this problem. It searches for the nearest neighbors in a higher dimensional space. For every application, it is important to define the meaning of similarity. The most popular definition is the Jaccard Similarity. It refers to the ratio between intersection sets and union. It is the best similarity to reveal textual similarity found in documents and certain behaviors of customers.

For example, when looking for identical documents, there are different instances of this particular example. There might be very many small pieces of one document appearing out of order, more documents for comparisons, and documents that are so large to fit in the main memory. To handle these issues, there are three important steps to finding similar documents.

- ***Shingling.*** This involves converting documents into sets.

- **Min-Hashing.** It involves converting a large set into short signatures while maintaining similarity.

- **Locality Sensitive Hashing.** Concentrate on signature pairs that might be from similar documents.

The most powerful way that you can represent documents assets is to retrieve a set of short strings from the document.

- A k-Shingle refers to any k characters that can show up in a document.
- A min-hash functions on sets.
- Locality-Sensitive Hashing.

3. Link Analysis

Traditional search engines did not provide accurate search results because of spam vulnerability. However, Google managed to overcome this problem by using the following technique:

- PageRank. It uses simulation. If a user surfing a web page starts from a random page, PageRank attempts to congregate in case it had monitored specific outlines from the page that users are located. This whole process works iteratively meaning pages that have a higher number of users are ranked better than pages without users visiting.

- The content in a page was determined by the specific phrases used in the page and linked with external pages. Although it is easy for a spammer to modify a page that they are administrators, it is very difficult for them to do the same on an external page which they aren't administrators.

In other words, PageRank represents a function that allocates a real number to a web page. The intention is that a page with a higher page rank becomes more important than a page that does not have a page rank. There is no fixed algorithm defined to assign a page rank, but there are different varieties.

For powerfully connected Web Graphs, PageRank applies the principle of the transition matrix. This principle is useful for calculating the rank of a page.

To calculate the behavior of a page rank, it simulates the actions of random users on a page.

There are different enhancements that one can make to PageRank. The first one is called Topic-Sensitive PageRank. This type of improvement can weigh certain pages more heavily as a result of their topic. If you are aware of the query on a particular page, then it is possible to be based on the rank of the page.

4. Data Streaming

In most of the Data Mining situations, you can't know the whole data set in advance. There are times when data arrives in the form of a stream, and then gets processed immediately before it disappears forever.

Furthermore, the speed at which data arrives very fast, and that makes it hard to store in the active storage. In short, the data is infinite and non-stationary. Stream management, therefore, becomes very important.

In the data stream management system, there is no limit to the number of streams that can fit into a system. Each data stream produces elements at its own time. The elements should then have the same data rates and time in a particular stream.

Streams can be archived into a store, but this will make it impossible to reply to queries from the archival store. This can later be analyzed under special cases by using a specific retrieval method.

Furthermore, there is a working store where summaries are placed so that one can use to reply to queries. The active store can either be a disk or main memory. It all depends on the speed at which one wants to process the queries. Whichever way, it does not have the right capacity to store data from other streams.

Data streaming has different problems as highlighted below:

- Sampling Data in a Stream

To create a sample of the stream that is used in a class of queries, you must select a set of attributes to be used in a stream. By hashing the key of an incoming stream element, the hash value can be the best to help determine whether all or none of the elements in the key belong to the sample.

- Filtering Streams

To accept tuples that fit a specific criterion, accepted tuples should go through a separate process of the stream while the rest of the tuples are eliminated. Bloom filtering is a wonderful technique that one can use to filter streams to allow elements in a given set to pass through while foreign elements are deleted.

Members in the selected set are hashed into buckets to form bits. The bits are then set to 1. If you would like to test an element of a stream, you must hash the element into a set of bits using the hash function.

- Count Specific Elements in a Stream

Consider stream elements chosen from a universal set. If you wanted to know the number of unique elements that exist in a stream, you might have to count from the start of the stream. Flajolet-Martin is a method which often hashes elements to integers, described as binary numbers. By using a lot of the hash functions and integrating these estimates, you finally get a reliable estimate.

5. Frequent Item – Set Analysis

The market-basket model features many relationships. On one side, there are items, and on the opposite side, there are baskets. Every basket contains a set of items. The hypothesis created here is that the number of items in the basket is always smaller than the total number of items. This means that if you count the items in the basket, it should be high and large to fit in memory. Here, data is similar to a file that has a series of baskets. In reference to the distributed file system, baskets represent the original file. Each basket is of type "set of items".

As a result, a popular family technique to characterize data depending on the market-basket model is to discover frequent item-sets. These are sets of items that reveal the most baskets.

Market basket analysis was previously applied in supermarket and chain stores. These stores track down the contents of each market basket that a customer brings to the checkout. Items represent products sold by the store while baskets are a set of items found in a single basket.

That said, this same model can be applied in many different data types such as:

• **Similar concepts.** Let items represent words and baskets documents. Therefore, a document or basket has words or items available in the document. If you were to search for words that are repeated in a document, sets would contain the most words.

• **Plagiarism.** You can let the items represent documents and baskets to be sentenced.

Properties of Frequent-Item Sets to Know

• **Association rules**. These refer to implications in case a basket has a specific set of items.

• **Monotonicity**. One of the most important properties of item-sets is that if a set is frequent, then all its subsets are frequent.

Part 2: DATA SCIENCE WITH PYTHON

Chapter 6. Introduction to NumPy

Now that you know the basics of loading and preprocessing data with the help of pandas, we can move on to data processing with NumPy. The purpose of this stage is to have a data matrix ready for the next stage, which involves supervised and unsupervised machine learning mechanisms. NumPy data structure comes in the form of ndarray objects, and this is what you will later feed into the machine learning process. For now, we will start by creating such an object to better understand this phase.

The n-dimensional Array

As we discussed in the chapter about Python fundamental data types, lists and dictionaries are some of Python's most important structures. You can build complex data structures with them because they are powerful at storing data, however they're not great at operating on that data. They aren't optimal when it comes to processing power and speed, which are critical when working with complex algorithms. This is why we're using NumPy and its ndarray object, which stands for an "n-dimensional array". Let's look at the properties of a NumPy array:

1. **It is optimal and fast at transferring data. When you work with complex data, you want the memory to handle it efficiently instead of being bottlenecked.**

2. **You can perform vectorization. In other words, you can make linear algebra computations and specific element operations without being forced to use "for" loops. This is a large plus for NumPy because Python "for" loops cost a lot of resources, making it really expensive to work with a large number of loops instead of ndarrays.**

3. In data science operations you will have to use tools, or libraries, such as SciPy and Scikit-learn. You can't use them without arrays because they are required as an input, otherwise functions won't perform as intended.

With that being said, here are a few methods of creating a ndarray:

1. Take an already existing data structure and turn into an array.
2. Build the array from the start and add in the values later.
3. You can also upload data to an array even when it's stored on a disk.

Converting a list to a one-dimensional array is a fairly common operation in data science processes. Keep in mind that you have to take into account the type of objects such a list contains. This will have an impact on the dimensionality of the result. Here's an example of this with a list that contains only integers:

In: import numpy as np

int_list = [1,2,3]

Array_1 = np.array(int_list)

In: Array_1

Out: array([1, 2, 3])

You can access the array just like you access a list in Python. You simply use indexing, and just like in Python, it starts from 0. This is how this operation would look:

In: Array_1[1]

Out: 2

Now you can gain more data about the objects inside the array like so:

In: type(Array_1)

Out: numpy.ndarray

In: Array_1.dtype

Out: dtype('int64')

The result of the dtype is related to the type of operating system you're running. In this example, we're using a 64 bit operating system.

At the end of this exercise, our basic list is transformed into a uni-dimensional array. But what happens if we have a list that contains more than just one type of element? Let's say we have integers, strings, and floats. Let's see an example of this:

In: import numpy as np

composite_list = [1,2,3] + [1.,2.,3.] + ['a','b','c']

Array_2 = np.array(composite_list[:3])#here we have only integers

print ('composite_list[:3]', Array_2.dtype)

Array_2 = np.array(composite _list[:6])   #now we have integers and floats

print (' composite _list[:6]', Array_2.dtype)

Array_2 = np.array(composite _list) #strings have been added to the array print (' composite _list[:] ',Array_2.dtype)

Out:

composite _list[:3] int64

composite _list[:6] float64

composite _list[:] <U32

As you can see, we have a "composite_list" that contains integers, floats, and strings. It's important to understand that when we make an array, we can have any kind of data types and mix them however we wish.

Next, let's see how we can load an array from a file. N-dimensional arrays can be created from the data contained inside a file. Here's an example in code:

In: import numpy as np

cars = np.loadtxt('regression-datasets

cars.csv',delimiter=',', dtype=float)

In this example, we tell our tool to create an array from a file with the help of the "loadtxt" method by giving it a filename, delimiter, and a data type.

Chapter 7. packages installations

To get started with NumPy, we have to install the package into our version of Python. While the basic method for installing packages to Python is the *pip install* method, we will be using the *conda install* method. This is the recommended way of managing all Python packages and virtual environments using the anaconda framework.

Since we installed a recent version of Anaconda, most of the packages we need would have been included in the distribution. To verify if any package is installed, you can use the *conda list* command via the anaconda prompt. This displays all the packages currently installed and accessible via anaconda. If your intended package is not available, then you can install via this method:

First, ensure you have an internet connection. This is required to download the target package via conda. Open the anaconda prompt, then enter the following code:

> Conda install **package**

Note: *In the code above, 'package' is what needs to be installed e.g. NumPy, Pandas, etc.*

As described earlier, we would be working with NumPy arrays. In programming, an array is an ordered collection of similar items. Sounds familiar? Yeah, they are just like Python lists, but with superpowers. NumPy arrays are in two forms: Vectors, and Matrices. They are mostly the same, only that vectors are one-dimensional arrays (either a column or a row of ordered items), while a matrix is 2-dimensional (rows and columns). These are the fundamental blocks of most operations we would be doing with NumPy. While arrays incorporate most of the operations possible with Python lists, we would be introducing some newer methods for creating, and manipulating them.

To begin using the NumPy methods, we have to first import the package into our current workspace. This can be achieved in two ways:

import numpy **as** np

Or

from numpy import *

In Jupyter notebook, enter either of the codes above to import the NumPy package. The first method of import is recommended, especially for beginners, as it helps to keep track of the specific package a called function/method is from. This is due to the variable assignment e.g. 'np', which refers to the imported package throughout the coding session.

Notice the use of an asterisk in the second import method. This signifies 'everything/all' in programming. Hence, the code reads **'from NumPy import everything!!'**

Tip: In Python, we would be required to reference the package we are operating with e.g. NumPy, Pandas, etc. It is easier to assign them variable names that can be used in further operations. This is significantly useful in a case where there are multiple packages being used, and the use of standard variable names such as: 'np' for NumPy, 'pd' for Pandas, etc. makes the code more readable.

Example: Creating vectors and matrices from Python lists.

Let us declare a Python list.

In []: # This is a list of integers
Int_list = [1,2,3,4,5]
    Int_list

Out[]: [1,2,3,4,5]

Importing the NumPy package and creating an array of integers.

In []: # import syntax
import numpy as np
np.array(Int_list)

Out[]: array([1, 2, 3, 4, 5])

Notice the difference in the outputs? The second output indicates that we have created an array, and we can easily assign this array to a variable for future reference.

To confirm, we can check for the type.

In []: x = np.array(Int_list)
    type(x)

Out[]: numpy.ndarray

We have created a vector, because it has one dimension (1 row). To check this, the 'ndim' method can be used.

In []: x.ndim   # this shows how many dimensions the array has
Out[]: 1

Alternatively, the shape method can be used to see the arrangements.

In []: x.shape   # this shows the shape

Out[]: (5,)

Python describes matrices as *(rows, columns)*. In this case, it describes a vector as *(number of elements,)*. To create a matrix from a Python list, we need to pass a nested list containing the elements we need. Remember, matrices are rectangular, and so each list in the nested list must have the same size.

In []: # This is a matrix

x = [1,2,3]
y = [4,5,6]

my_list = [y,x]   # nested list

my_matrix = np.array(my_list)   # creating the matrix

A = my_matrix.ndim
B = my_matrix.shape

# Printing
print('Resulting matrix:\n\n',my_matrix,'\n\nDimensions:',A, '\nshape (rows,columns):',B)

Out[]: Resulting matrix:

[[4 5 6]
 [1 2 3]]

Dimensions: 2

shape (rows,columns): (2, 3)

Now, we have created a 2 by 3 matrix. Notice how the shape method displays the rows and columns of the matrix. To find the transpose of this matrix i.e. change the rows to columns, use the ***transpose ()*** method.

```
In []: # this finds the transpose of the matrix
t_matrix = my_matrix.transpose()
       t_matrix

Out[]: array([[4, 1],
       [5, 2],
       [6, 3]])
```

Tip: *Another way of knowing the number of dimensions of an array is by counting the square-brackets that opens and closes the array (immediately after the parenthesis). In the vector example, notice that the array was enclosed in single square brackets. In the two-dimensional array example, however, there are two brackets. Also, tuples can be used in place of lists for creating arrays.*

There are other methods of creating arrays in Python, and they may be more intuitive than using lists in some applications. One quick method uses the ***arange()*** function.

Syntax: np.arange(start value, stop value, step size, dtype = 'type')
In this case, we do not need to pass its output to the list function, our result is an array object of a data type specified by 'dtype'.

Example: Creating arrays with the arange() function.

We will create an array of numbers from 0 to 10, with an increment of 2 (even numbers).

In []: # Array of even numbers between 0 and 10
Even_array = np.arange(0,11,2)
Even_array

Out[]: array([0, 2, 4, 6, 8, 10])

Notice it behaves like the range () method form our list examples. It returned all even values between 0 and 11 (10 being the maximum). Here, we did not specify the types of the elements.

Tip: *Recall, the range method returns value up to the 'stop value – 1'; hence, even if we change the 11 to 12, we would still get 10 as the maximum.*

Since the elements are numeric, they can either be integers or floats. Integers are the default, however, to return the values as floats, we can also specify the numeric type.

In []: Even_array2 = np.arange(0,11,2, dtype='float')
Even_array2

Out[]: array([0., 2., 4., 6., 8., 10.])

Another handy function for creating arrays is *linspace()*. This returns a numeric array of linearly space values within an interval. It also allows for the specification of the required number of points, and it has the following syntax:

np.linspace(start value, end value, number of points)

At default, linspace returns an array of 50 evenly spaced points within the defined interval.

Example: Creating arrays of evenly spaced points with linspace()

In []: # Arrays of linearly spaced points
A = np.linspace(0,5,5) # 5 equal points between 0 & 5
B = np.linspace (51,100) # 50 equal points between 51 & 100

    print ('Here are the arrays:\n')

A
B

Here are the arrays:

Out[ ]: array([0. , 1.25, 2.5 , 3.75, 5.])
Out[ ]: array([1., 2., 3., 4., 5., 6., 7., 8., 9., 10., 11., 12., 13., 14.,
        15., 16., 17., 18., 19., 20., 21., 22., 23., 24., 25., 26., 27.,
        28., 29., 30., 31., 32., 33., 34., 35., 36., 37., 38., 39., 40.,
        41., 42., 43., 44., 45., 46., 47., 48., 49., 50.])

Notice how the second use of linspace did not require a third argument. This is because we wanted 50 equally spaced values, which is the default. The 'dtype' can also be specified like we did with the range function.

Tip 1: *Linspace arrays are particularly useful in plots. They can be used to create a time axis or any other required axis for producing well defined and scaled graphs.*

Tip 2: *The output format in the example above is not the default way for output in Jupyter notebook. Jupyter displays the last result per cell, at default. To display multiple results (without having to use the print statement every-time), the output method can be*

changed using the following code.
In[]: # Allowing Jupyter output all results per cell.
run the following code in a Jupyter cell.

```
from IPython.core.interactiveshell import InteractiveShell
InteractiveShell.ast_node_interactivity = "all"
```

There are times when a programmer needs unique arrays like the identity matrix, or a matrix of ones/zeros. NumPy provides a convenient way of creating these with the *zeros()*, *ones()* and *eye()* functions.

Example: creating arrays with unique elements.

Let us use the zeros () function to create a vector and a matrix.

```
In []: np.zeros(3)   # A vector of 3 elements
np.zeros((2,3)) # A matrix of 6 elements i.e. 2 rows, 3 columns
```

Out[]: array([0., 0., 0.])
Out[]: array([[0., 0., 0.],
   [0., 0., 0.]])

Notice how the second output is a two-dimensional array i.e. two square brackets (a matrix of 2 columns and 3 rows as specified in the code).

The same thing goes for creating a vector or matrix with all elements having a value of '1'.

```
In []: np.ones(3)   # A vector of 3 elements
```

```
np.ones((2,3)) # A matrix of 6 elements i.e. 2 rows, 3 columns
```

Out[]: array([1., 1., 1.])
Out[]: array([[1., 1., 1.],
    [1., 1., 1.]])

Also, notice how the code for creating the matrices requires the row and column instructions to be passed as a tuple. This is because the function accepts one input, so multiple inputs would need to be passed as tuples or lists in the required order (Tuples are recommended. Recall, they are faster to operate.).

In the case of the identity matrix, the function eye () only requires one value. Since identity matrices are always square, the value passed determines the number of rows and columns.

```
In []: np.eye(2)  # A matrix of 4 elements 2 rows, 2 columns
np.eye(3)  # 3 rows, 3 columns
```

Out[]: array([[1., 0.],
    [0., 1.]])
Out[]: array([[1., 0., 0.],
    [0., 1., 0.],
    [0., 0., 1.]])

NumPy also features random number generators. These can be used for creating arrays, as well as single values, depending on the required application. To access the random number generator, we call the library via ***np.random***, and then choose the random method we prefer. We will consider three methods for generating random numbers: ***rand()***, ***randn()***, and ***randint()***.

Example: Generating arrays with random values.

Let us start with the rand () method. This generates random, uniformly distributed numbers between 0 and 1.

```
In []: np.random.rand (2)    # A vector of 2 random values
       np.random.rand (2,3)  # A matrix of 6 random values

Out[]: array([0.01562571, 0.54649508])
Out[]: array([[0.22445055, 0.35909056, 0.53403529],
       [0.70449515, 0.96560456, 0.79583743]])
```

Notice how each value within the arrays are between 0 & 1. You can try this on your own and observe the returned values. Since it is a random generation, these values may be different from yours. Also, in the case of the random number generators, the matrix specifications are not required to be passed as lists or tuples, as observed in the second line of code.

The randn () method generates random numbers from the standard normal or Gaussian distribution. You might want to brush up on some basics in statistics, however, this just implies that the values returned would have a tendency towards the mean (which is zero in this case) i.e. the values would be centered around zero.

```
In []: np.random.randn (2)    # A vector of 2 random values
       np.random.randn (2,3)  # A matrix of 6 random values

Out[]: array([ 0.73197866, -0.31538023])
Out[]: array([[-0.79848228, -0.7176693 , 0.74770505],
       [-2.10234448, 0.10995745, -0.54636425]])
```

The randint() method generates random integers within a specified range or interval. Note that the higher range value is exclusive (i.e.

has no chance of being randomly selected), while the lower value is inclusive (could be included in the random selection).

Syntax: np.random(lower value, higher value, number of values, dtype)
If the number of values is not specified, Python just returns a single value within the defined range.

```
In []: np.random.randint (1,5)      # A random value between 1 and 5
 np.random.randint (1,100,6)   # A vector of 6 random values
 np.random.randint (1,100,(2,3)) # A matrix of 6 random values
Out[]: 4
Out[]: array([74, 42, 92, 10, 76, 43])
Out[]: array([[92,  9, 99],
       [73, 36, 93]])
```

Tip: Notice how the size parameter for the third line was specified using a tuple. This is how to create a matrix of random integers using randint.

Example: Illustrating randint().

Let us create a fun dice roll program using the randint() method. We would allow two dice, and the function will return an output based on the random values generated in the roll.

In []: # creating a dice roll game with randint()
```
# Defining the function
def roll_dice():
    """ This function displays a
    dice roll value when called"""

    dice1 = np.random.randint(1,7) # This allows 6 to be inclusive
    dice2 = np.random.randint(1,7)

# Display Condition.
    if dice1 == dice2:
  print('Roll: ',dice1,'&',dice2,'\ndoubles !')
        if dice1 == 1:
            print('snake eyes!\n')
        else:
   print('Roll: ',dice1,'&',dice2)
```

In []: # Calling the function
```
roll_dice()
```

Out[]: Roll: 1 & 1
doubles !

snake eyes!

Hint: *Think of a fun and useful program to illustrate the use of these random number generators, and writing such programs will improve your chances of comprehension. Also, a quick review of statistics, especially measures of central tendency & dispersion/spread will be useful in your data science journey.*

Chapter 8. manipulating array

Now that we have learned how to declare arrays, we would be proceeding with some methods for modifying these arrays. First, we will consider the ***reshape ()*** method, which is used for changing the dimensions of an array.

Example: Using the reshape() method.

Let us declare a few arrays and call the reshape method to change their dimensions.

In []: freq = np.arange(10);values = np.random.randn(10)
   freq; values

Out[]: array([0, 1, 2, 3, 4, 5, 6, 7, 8, 9])

Out[]: array([1.33534821, 1.73863505, 0.1982571 , -0.47513784,
   1.80118596,   -1.73710743,
   -0.24994721, 1.41695744, -0.28384007, 0.58446065])

Using the reshape method, we would make 'freq' and 'values' 2 dimensional.

In []: np.reshape(freq,(5,2))

Out[]: array([[0, 1],
   [2, 3],
   [4, 5],
   [6, 7],
   [8, 9]])

In []: np.reshape(values,(2,5))

Out[]: array([[1.33534821, 1.73863505, 0.1982571 , -0.47513784,
        1.80118596],
        [-1.73710743, -0.24994721, 1.41695744, -0.28384007,
        0.58446065]])

Even though the values array still looks similar after reshaping, notice the two square brackets that indicate it has been changed to a matrix. The reshape method comes in handy when we need to do array operations, and our arrays are inconsistent in dimensions. It is also important to ensure the new size parameter passed to the reshape method does not differ from the number of elements in the original array. The idea is simple: when calling the reshape method, the product of the size parameters must equal the number of elements in the original array.

The maximum and minimum values within an array (or real-world data), and possibly the index of such maximum or minimum values. To get this information, we can use the *.max()*, *.min()*, *.argmax()* and *.argmin()* methods respectively.

Example:
Let us find the maximum and minimum values in the 'values' array, along with the index of the minimum and maximum within the array.

In []: A = values.max();B = values.min();
    C = values.argmax()+1; D = values.argmin()+1

    print('Maximum value: {}\nMinimum Value: {}\
    \nItem {} is the maximum value, while item {}\
    is the minimum value'.format(A,B,C,D))

Output

Maximum value: 1.8011859577930067
Minimum Value: -1.7371074259180737

Item 5 is the maximum value, while item 6 is the minimum value

A few things to note in the code above: The variables C&D, which defines the position of the maximum and minimum values are evaluated as shown [by adding 1 to the index of the maximum and minimum values obtained via **argmax ()** and **argmin ()**], because Python indexing starts at zero. Python would index maximum value at 4, and minimum at 5, which is not the actual positions of these elements within the array (you are less likely to start counting elements in a list from zero! Unless you are Python, of course.).

Another observation can be made in the code. The print statement is broken across a few lines using enter. To allow Python to know that the next line of code is a continuation, the backslash '\' is used. Another way would be to use three quotes for a multiline string.

Chapter 9. conditional selection,

Similar to how we conditional selection works with NumPy arrays, we can select elements from a data frame that satisfy a Boolean criterion.

Example: Let us grab sections of the data frame 'Arr_df' where the value is > 5.

In []: # Grab elements greater than five

Arr_df[Arr_df>5]

Output:

	odd1	even1	odd2	even2	Odd sum	Even sum
A	NaN	NaN	NaN	NaN	NaN	6
B	NaN	6.0	7.0	8.0	12.0	14
C	9.0	10.0	11.0	12.0	20.0	22
D	13.0	14.0	15.0	16.0	28.0	30
E	17.0	18.0	19.0	20.0	36.0	38

Notice how the instances of values less than 5 are represented with a 'NaN'.

Another way to use this conditional formatting is to format based on column specifications.

You could remove entire rows of data, by specifying a Boolean condition based off a single column. Assuming we want to return the Arr_df data frame without the row 'C'. We can specify a condition to return values where the elements of column 'odd1' are not equal to '9' (since row C contains 9 under column 'odd1').

```
In []: # removing row C through the first column
    Arr_df[Arr_df['odd1']!= 9]
```

Output:

	odd1	even1	odd2	even2	Odd sum	Even sum
A	1	2	3	4	4	6
B	5	6	7	8	12	14
D	13	14	15	16	28	30
E	17	18	19	20	36	38

Notice that row 'C' has been filtered out. This can be achieved through a smart conditional statement through any of the columns.

```
In []:  # does the same thing : remove row 'C'
     # Arr_df[Arr_df['even2']!= 12]

In[]: # Let us remove rows D and E through 'even2'
    Arr_df[Arr_df['even2']<= 12]
```

Output

	odd1	even1	odd2	even2	Odd sum	Even sum
A	1	2	3	4	4	6
B	5	6	7	8	12	14
C	9	10	11	12	20	22

Exercise: Remove rows C, D, E via the 'Even sum' column. Also, try out other such operations as you may prefer.

To combine conditional selection statements, we can use the 'logical and, i.e. &', and the 'logical or, i.e. |' for nesting multiple conditions. The regular 'and' and 'or' operators would not work in this case as they are used for comparing single elements. Here, we will be comparing a series of elements that evaluate to true or false, and those generic operators find such operations ambiguous.

Example: Let us select elements that meet the criteria of being greater than 1 in the first column, and less than 22 in the last column. Remember, the 'and statement' only evaluates to true if both conditions are true.

In []:Arr_df[(Arr_df['odd1']>1) & (Arr_df['Even sum']<22)]

Output:

	odd1	even1	odd2	even2	Odd sum	Even sum
B	5	6	7	8	12	14

Only the elements in Row 'B' meet this criterion, and were returned in the data frame.

This approach can be expounded upon to create even more powerful data frame filters.

Chapter 10. NumPy Array Operations,

Sometimes, when you work with two dimensional arrays, you may want to add new rows or columns to represent new data and variables. This operation is known as array stacking, and it doesn't take long for NumPy to render the new information. Start by creating a new array:

In: import numpy as np

dataset = np.arange(50).reshape(10,5)

Next, add a new row, and several lines that will be concatenated:

In: single_line = np.arange(1*5).reshape(1,5)

several_lines = np.arange(3*5).reshape(3,5)

Now let's use the vstack method, which stands for vertical stack, to add a new single line.

In: np.vstack((dataset,single_line))

This command line will also work if we want to add several lines.

In: np.vstack((dataset,several_lines))

Next, let's see how to add a variable to the array. This is done with the "hstack" method, which stands for horizontal stack. Here's an example:

In: bias = np.ones(10).reshape(10,1) np.hstack((dataset,bias))

In this line of code, we added a bias of unit values to the array we created earlier.

As an aspiring data scientist, you will only need to know how to add new rows and columns to your arrays. In most projects you won't need to do more than that, so practice working with two dimensional arrays and NumPy, because this tool is engraved in data science.

Chapter 11. Pandas,

Pandas is built on NumPy and they are meant to be used together. This makes it extremely easy to extract arrays from the data frames. Once these arrays are extracted, they can be turned into data frames themselves. Let's take a look at an example:

In: import pandas as pd

import numpy as np

marketing_filename = 'regression-datasets-marketing.csv'

marketing = pd.read_csv(marketing_filename, header=None)

In this phase we are uploading data to a data frame. Next, we're going to use the "values" method in order to extract an array that is of the same type as those contained inside the data frame.

In: marketing_array = marketing.values

marketing_array.dtype

Out: dtype('float64')

We can see that we have a float type array. You can anticipate the type of the array by first using the "dtype" method. This will establish which types are being used by the specified data frame object. Do this before extracting the array. This is how this operation would look:

In: marketing.dtypes

Out: 0float64

1 int64

2   float64

3   int64

4   float64

5   float64

6   float64

7   float64

8   int64

9   int64

10   int64

11   float64

12   float64

13   float64

dtype: object

Matrix Operations

This includes matrix calculations, such as matrix to matrix multiplication. Let's create a two dimensional array.

This is a two dimensional array of numbers from 0 to 24. Next, we will declare a vector of coefficients and a column that will stack the vector and its reverse. Here's what it would look like:

In: coefs = np.array([1., 0.5, 0.5, 0.5, 0.5])

coefs_matrix = np.column_stack((coefs,coefs[::-1]))

print (coefs_matrix)

Out:

[[1. 0.5]

[0.5 0.5]

[0.5 0.5]

[0.5 0.5]

[0.5 1.]]

Now we can perform the multiplication. Here's an example of multiplying the array with the vector:

In: np.dot(M,coefs)

Out: array([5.,20.,35.,50.,65.])

Here's an example of multiplication between the array and the coefficient vectors:

In: np.dot(M,coefs_matrix)

Out:array([[5.,7.],

[20.,22.],

[35.,37.],

[50.,52.],

[65.,67.]])

In both of these multiplication operations, we used the "np.dot" function in order to achieve them. Next up, let's discuss slicing and indexing.

Slicing and Indexing

Indexing is great for viewing the ndarray by sending an instruction to visualize the slice of columns and rows or the index.

Let's start by creating a 10x10 array. It will initially be two-dimensional.

In: import numpy as np

M = np.arange(100, dtype=int).reshape(10,10)

Next let's extract the rows from 2 to 8, but only the ones that are evenly numbered.

In: M[2:9:2,:]

Out:array([[20, 21, 22, 23, 24, 25, 26, 27, 28, 29],

[40, 41, 42, 43, 44, 45, 46, 47, 48, 49],

[60, 61, 62, 63, 64, 65, 66, 67, 68, 69],

[80, 81, 82, 83, 84, 85, 86, 87, 88, 89]])

Now let's extract the column, but only the ones from index 5.

In: M[2:9:2,5:]

Out:array([[25, 26, 27, 28, 29],

[45, 46, 47, 48, 49],

[65, 66, 67, 68, 69],

[85, 86, 87, 88, 89]])

We successfully sliced the rows and the columns. But what happens if we try a negative index? Doing so would reverse the array. Here's how our previous array would look when using a negative index.

In: M[2:9:2,5::-1]

Out:array([[25, 24, 23, 22, 21, 20],

[45, 44, 43, 42, 41, 40],

[65, 64, 63, 62, 61, 60],

[85, 84, 83, 82, 81, 80]])

There are other ways of slicing and indexing the arrays, but for the purposes of this book it's enough to know how to perform the previously mentioned steps. However, keep in mind that this process is only a way of viewing the data. If you want to use these views further by creating new data, you cannot make any modifications in the original arrays. If you do, it can lead to some negative side effects. In that case, you want to use the "copy" method. This will create a copy of the array which you can modify however you wish. Here's the code line for the copy method:

In: N = M[2:9:2,5:].copy()

Chapter 12. Data frames,

A Pandas data frame is just an ordered collection of Pandas series with a common/shared index. At its basic form, a data frame looks more like an excel sheet with rows, columns, labels and headers. To create a data frame, the following syntax is used:

> pd.DataFrame(data=None, index=None, columns=None, dtype=None, copy=False)

Usually, the data input is an array of values (of whatever datatype). The index and column parameters are usually lists/vectors of either numeric or string type.

If a Pandas series is passed to a data frame object, the index automatically becomes the columns, and the data points are assigned accordingly.

Example: Creating a data frame

```
In []: df = pd.DataFrame([pool1])     # passing a series
df                    # show

# two series
index = 'WWI WWII'.split()
new_df = pd.DataFrame([pool1,pool3],index)
new_df                # show
```

Output:

USA	Britain	France	Germany
0	1	2	3	4

	USA	Britain	France	Germany
WWI	1	2	3	4
WWII	5	1	3	4

We have created two data frames from the pool 1 and pool 3 series we created earlier. Notice how the first data frame assigns the series labels as column headers, and since no index was assigned, a value of '0' was set at that index i.e. row header.

For the second data frame, the row labels were specified by passing a list of strings ['WWI','WWII'].

*Tip: The **.split()** string method is a quick way of creating lists of strings. It works by splitting a string into its component characters, depending on the delimiter passed to the string method.*

For example, let us split this email 'pythonguy@gmail.com' into a list containing the username and the domain name.

```
In []:  # Illustrating the split() method

email = 'pythonguy@gmail.com'
string_vec = email.split('@')
string_vec     # show
A = string_vec[0]; B = string_vec[1] # Extracting values
print('Username:',A,'\nDomain name:',B)

Out[]: ['pythonguy', 'gmail.com']
   Username: pythonguy
   Domain name: gmail.com
```

To create a data frame with an array, we can use the following method:

```
# Creating dataframe with an array

Array = np.arange(1,21).reshape(5,4)  # numpy array
row_labels = 'A B C D E'.split()
col_labels = 'odd1 even1 odd2 even2'.split()
Arr_df = pd.DataFrame(Array,row_labels,col_labels)
Arr_df
```

Output:

	odd1	even1	odd2	even2
A	1	2	3	4
B	5	6	7	8
C	9	10	11	12
D	13	14	15	16
E	17	18	19	20

Notice how this is not unlike how we create spreadsheets in excel. Try playing around with creating data frames.

Exercise: Create a data frame from a 5 × 4 array of uniformly distributed random values. Include your choice row and column names using the *.split()* method.

Hint: use the rand function to generate your values, and use the reshape method to form an array.

Now that we can conveniently create Data frames, we are going to learn how to index and grab elements off them.

Tip: Things to note about data frames.

- *They are a collection of series (more like a list with Pandas series as its elements).*

- *They are similar to numpy arrays i.e. they are more like n × m dimensional matrices, where 'n' are the rows and 'm' are the columns.*

Example: Grabbing elements from a data frame.

The easiest elements to grab are the columns. This is because, by default, each column element is a series with the row headers as labels. We can grab them by using a similar method from the series – indexing by name.

In []: # Grab data frame elements

Arr_df['odd1']   # grabbing first column

Out[]: A   1
B   5
C   9
D   13
E   17
Name: odd1, dtype: int32

Pretty easy, right? Notice how the output is like a Pandas series. You can verify this by using the ***type(Arr_df['odd1'])*** command.

When more than one column is grabbed, however, it returns a data frame (which makes sense, since a data frame is a collection of at least two series). To grab more than one column, pass the column names to the indexing as a list. This is shown in the example code below:

In []:# Grab two columns

Arr_df[['odd1','even2']] # grabbing first and last columns

Output:

	odd1	even2
A	1	4
B	5	8
C	9	12
D	13	16
E	17	20

To select a specific element, use the double square brackets indexing notation we learned under array indexing. For example, let us select the value 15 from Arr_df.

In []: Arr_df['odd2']['D']
Out[]: 15

You may decide to break the steps into two, if it makes it easier. This method is however preferred as it saves memory from variable allocation. To explain, let us break it down into two steps.

In []: x = Arr_df['odd2']
x

```
Out[]: A    3
       B    7
       C    11
       D    15
       E    19
       Name: odd2, dtype: int32
```

See that the first operation returns a series containing the element '15'. This series can now be indexed to grab 15 using the label 'D'.

```
In []: x['D']
Out[]: 15
```

While this approach works, and is preferred by beginners, a better approach is to get comfortable with the first method to save coding time and resources.

To grab rows, a different indexing method is used. You can use either *data_frame_name.loc['row_name']* or *data_frame_name.iloc['row_index']*.

Let us grab the row E from *Arr_df*.

```
In []: print("using .loc['E']")
   Arr_df.loc['E']

   print('\nusing .iloc[4]')
   Arr_df.iloc[4]

   using .loc['E']
```

Out[]:
    odd1   17
    even1   18
    odd2   19
    even2   20
    Name: E, dtype: int32

    using .iloc[4]
Out[]:
    odd1   17
    even1   18
    odd2   19
    even2   20
    Name: E, dtype: int32

See, the same result!

You can also use the row indexing method to select single items.

```
In []: Arr_df.loc['E']['even2']
    # or
    Arr_df.iloc[4]['even2']

Out[]: 20

Out[]: 20
```

Moving on, we will try to create new columns in a data frame, and also delete a column.

```
In []: # Let us add two sum columns to Arr_df

Arr_df['Odd sum'] = Arr_df['odd1']+Arr_df['odd2']
Arr_df['Even sum'] = Arr_df['even1']+Arr_df['even2']
```

Arr_df

Output:

	odd1	even1	odd2	even2	Odd sum	Even sum
A	1	2	3	4	4	6
B	5	6	7	8	12	14
C	9	10	11	12	20	22
D	13	14	15	16	28	30
E	17	18	19	20	36	38

Notice how the new columns are declared. Also, arithmetic operations are possible with each element in the data frame, just like we did with the series.

Exercise: Add an extra column to this data frame. Call it Total Sum, and it should be the addition of Odd sum and Even sum.

To remove a column from a data frame, we use the *data_frame_name.drop()* method.

Let us remove the insert a new column and then remove it using the *.drop()* method.

In []: Arr_df['disposable'] = np.zeros(5)   # **new column**
　　　Arr_df **#show**

Output:

	odd1	even1	odd2	even2	Odd sum	Even sum	disposable
A	1	2	3	4	4	6	0.0
B	5	6	7	8	12	14	0.0
C	9	10	11	12	20	22	0.0
D	13	14	15	16	28	30	0.0
E	17	18	19	20	36	38	0.0

To remove the unwanted column:

```
In []: # to remove
Arr_df.drop('disposable',axis=1,inplace=True)
Arr_df
```

Output:

	odd1	even1	odd2	even2	Odd sum	Even sum
A	1	2	3	4	4	6
B	5	6	7	8	12	14
C	9	10	11	12	20	22

D	13	14	15	16	28	30
E	17	18	19	20	36	38

Notice the 'axis=1' and 'inplace = True' arguments. These are parameters that specify the location to perform the drop i.e. axis (axis = 0 specifies row operation), and intention to broadcast the drop to the original data frame, respectively. If 'inplace= False', the data frame will still contain the dropped column.

Chapter 13. Missing Data,

There are instances when the data being imported or generated into pandas is incomplete or have missing data points. In such a case, the likely solution is to remove such values from the dataset, or to fill in new values based on some statistical extrapolation techniques. While we would not be fully exploring statistical measures of extrapolation (you can read up on that from any good statistics textbook), we would be considering the use of the *.dropna()* and *.fillna()* methods for removing and filling up missing data points respectively.

To illustrate this, we will create a data frame – to represent imported data with missing values, and then use these two data preparation methods on it.

Example: Another way to create a data frame is by using a dictionary. Remember, a python dictionary is somehow similar to a Pandas series in that they have key-value pairs, just as Pandas series are label-value pairs (although this is a simplistic comparison for the sake of conceptualization).

```
In []:# First, our dictionary
dico = {'X':[1,2,np.nan],'Y':[4,np.nan,np.nan],'Z':[7,8,9]}
dico #show

# passing the dictionary to a dataframe
row_labels = 'A B C'.split()
df = pd.DataFrame(dico,row_labels)
df #show
```

Output:

{'X': [1, 2, nan], 'Y': [4, nan, nan], 'Z': [7, 8, 9]}

	X	Y	Z
A	1.0	4.0	7
B	2.0	NaN	8
C	NaN	NaN	9

Now, let us start off with the *.dropna()* method. This removes any 'null' or 'nan' values in the data frame it's called off, either column-wise or row-wise, depending on the axis specification and other arguments passed to the method. It has the following default syntax:

df.dropna(axis=0, how='any', thresh=None, subset=None, inplace=False)

The 'df' above is the data frame name. The default axis is set to zero, which represent row-wise operation. Hence, at default, the method will remove any row containing 'nan' values.

Let us see what happens when we call this method for our data frame.

In []: # this removes 'nan' row-wise
    df.dropna()

Output:	X	Y	Z
A	1.0	4.0	7

Notice that rows B and C contain at least a 'nan' value. Hence, they were removed.

Let us try a column-wise operation by specifying the axis=1.

```
In []: # this removes 'nan' column-wise
    df.dropna(axis=1)
```

Output:

	Z
A	7
B	8
C	9

As expected, only the column 'Z' was returned.

Now, in case we want to set a condition for a minimum number of 'non-nan' values/ actual data points required to make the cut (or escape the cut, depending on your perspective), we can use the 'thresh' (short for threshold) parameter to specify this.

Say, we want to remove 'nan' row-wise, but we only want to remove instances where the row had more than one actual data point value. We can set the threshold to 2 as illustrated in the following code:

```
In []: # drop rows with less than 2 actual values
    df.dropna(thresh = 2)
```

Output:

	X	Y	Z
A	1.0	4.0	7
B	2.0	NaN	8

Notice how we have filtered out row C, since it contains only one actual value '9'.

Exercise: Filter out columns in the data frame 'df' containing less than 2 actual data points

Next, let us use the *.fillna()* method to replace the missing values with our extrapolations.

Let us go ahead and replace our 'NaN' values with an 'x' marker. We can specify the 'X' as a string, and pass it into the 'value' parameter in *.fillna()*.

In []: # filling up NaNs
df.fillna('X')

Output:

	X	Y	Z
A	1	4	7
B	2	X	8

| C | X | X | 9 |

While marking missing data with an 'X' is fun, it is sometimes more intuitive (for lack of a better statistical approach), to use the mean of the affected column as a replacement for the missing elements.

Chapter 14. Group-By

This Pandas method, as the name suggests, allows the grouping of related data to perform combined/aggregate operations on them.

XYZ sales information

	Sales Person	Product	Sales
1	Sam	Hp	200
2	Charlie	Hp	120
3	Amy	Apple	340
4	Vanessa	Apple	124
5	Carl	Dell	243
6	Sarah	Dell	350

From our dataset, we can observe some common items under the product column. This is an example of an entry point for the group-by method in a data set. We can find information about the sales using the product grouping.

In []: # finding sales information by product

print('Total items sold: by product')

df.groupby('Product').sum()

Total items sold: by product

Product	Sales
Apple	464
Dell	593
Hp	320

This is an example of an aggregate operation using groupby. Other functions can be called to display interesting results as well. For example, *.count()*:

In []: df.groupby('Product').count()

Output:

Product	Sales Person	Sales
Apple	2	2
Dell	2	2
Hp	2	2

While the previous operation could not return the 'Sales person' field, since a numeric operation like 'sum' cannot be performed on a string, the count method returns the instances of each product within both categories. Via this output, we can easily infer that XYZ company assigns two salespersons per product, and that each of the sales persons made a sale of the products. However, unlike the sum method, this count method does not give a clearer overview of the sales. This is why so many methods are usually called to explain certain aspects of data. A very useful method for checking multiple information at a time is the .describe() method.

In []: #Getting better info using describe ()
     df.groupby('Product').describe()

Output:

Product		Sales							
	count	mean	std	min	25%	50%	75%	max
Apple	2.0	232.0	152.735065	124.0	178.00	232.0	286.00	340.0
Dell	2.0	296.5	75.660426	243.0	269.75	296.5	323.25	350.0
Hp	2.0	160.0	56.568542	120.0	140.00	160.0	180.00	200.0

Now, this is more informative. It says a lot about the data at a glance. Individual products can also be selected: df.groupby('Product').describe()['Product name e.g. 'Apple'].

77

Chapter 15. Reading and writing data

In real-world applications, data comes in various formats. These are the most common ones: CSV, Excel spreadsheets (xlsx / xls), HTML and SQL. While Pandas can read SQL files, it is not necessarily the best for working with SQL databases, since there are quite a few SQL engines: SQL lite, PostgreSQL, MySQL, etc. Hence, we will only be considering CSV, Excel and HTML.

Read

The *pd.read_file_type('file_name')* method is the default way to read files into the Pandas framework. After import, pandas displays the content as a data frame for manipulation using all the methods we have practiced so far, and more.

CSV (comma separated variables) & Excel

Create a CSV file in excel and save it in your python directory. You can check where your python directory is in Jupyter notebook by typing: *pwd()*. If you want to change to another directory containing your files (e.g. Desktop), you can use the following code:

```
In []: import os
os.chdir('C:\\Users\\Username\\Desktop')
```

To import your CSV file, type: pd.read_csv('csv_file_name'). Pandas will automatically detect the data stored in the file and display it as a data frame. A better approach would be to assign the imported data to a variable like this:

```
In []: Csv_data = pd.read_csv('example file.csv')
    Csv_data         # show
```

Running this cell will assign the data in 'example file.csv' to the variable Csv_data, which is of the type data frame. Now it can be called later or used for performing some of the data frame operations.

For excel files (.xlsx and .xls files), the same approach is taken. To read an excel file named 'class data.xlsx', we use the following code:

In []:Xl_data = pd.read_excel('class data.xlsx')
    Xl_data   # show

This returns a data frame of the required values. You may notice that an index starting from 0 is automatically assigned at the left side. This is similar to declaring a data frame without explicitly including the index field. You can add index names, like we did in previous examples.

Tip: in case the excel spreadsheet has multiple sheets filled. You can specify the sheet you need to be imported. Say we need only sheet 1, we use: *sheetname = 'Sheet 1'*. For extra functionality, you may check the documentation for *read_excel()* by using *shift+tab*.

Write

After working with our imported or pandas-built data frames, we can write the resulting data frame back into various formats. We will, however, only consider writing back to CSV and excel. To write a data frame to CSV, use the following syntax:

In []:Csv_data.to_csv('**file name**',index = False)

This writes the data frame 'Csv_data' to a CSV file with the specified filename in the python directory. If the file does not exist, it creates it.

For writing to an excel file, a similar syntax is used, but with sheet name specified for the data frame being exported.

In []:   Xl_data.to_excel('file name.xlsx',sheet_name = 'Sheet 1')

This writes the data frame *Xl_data* to sheet one of *'file name.xlsx'*.

Html

Reading Html files through pandas requires a few libraries to be installed: htmllib5, lxml, and BeautifulSoup4. Since we installed the latest Anaconda, these libraries are likely to be included. Use *conda list* to verify, and *conda install* to install any missing ones.

Html tables can be directly read into pandas using the ***pd.read_html** ('sheet url')* method. The sheet url is a web link to the data set to be imported. As an example, let us import the 'Failed bank lists' dataset from FDIC's website and call it w_data.

In []:   w_data = pd.read_html('http://www.fdic.gov/bank/individual/failed/banklist.html')

w_data[0]

To display the result, here we used *w_data [0]*. This is because the table we need is the first sheet element in the webpage source code. If you are familiar with HTML, you can easily identify where each element lies. To inspect a web page source code, use Chrome browser. ***On the web page >> right click >> then, select 'view page source'.*** Since what we are looking for is a table-like data, it will be specified like that in the source code. For example, here is where the data set is created in the FDIC page source code:

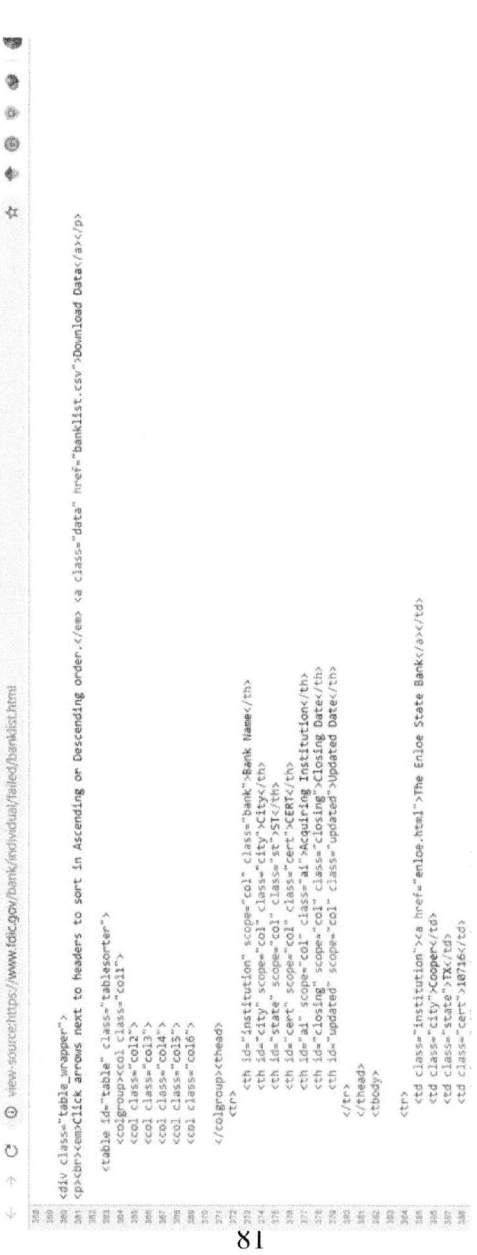

```html
<div class="table_wrapper">
<p><br><em>Click arrows next to headers to sort in Ascending or Descending order.</em> <a class="data" href="banklist.csv">Download Data</a></p>
<table id="table" class="tablesorter">
  <colgroup><col class="col1">
  <col class="col2">
  <col class="col3">
  <col class="col4">
  <col class="col5">
  <col class="col6">
  </colgroup><thead>
    <tr>
      <th id="institution" scope="col" class="bank">Bank Name</th>
      <th id="city" scope="col" class="city">City</th>
      <th id="state" scope="col" class="st">ST</th>
      <th id="cert" scope="col" class="cert">CERT</th>
      <th id="ai" scope="col" class="ai">Acquiring Institution</th>
      <th id="closing" scope="col" class="closing">Closing Date</th>
      <th id="updated" scope="col" class="updated">Updated Date</th>
    </tr>
  </thead>
  <tbody>
    <tr>
      <td class="institution"><a href="enloe.html">The Enloe State Bank</a></td>
      <td class="city">Cooper</td>
      <td class="state">TX</td>
      <td class="cert">10716</td>
```

FDIC page source via chrome

This section concludes our lessons on the Pandas framework. To test your knowledge on all that has been introduced, ensure to attempt all the exercises below. In the next chapter, we will be exploring some data visualization frameworks.

For the exercise, we will be working on an example dataset. A salary spreadsheet from Kaggle.com. Go ahead and download the spreadsheet from this link: www.kaggle.com/kaggle/sf-salaries

Note: **You might be required to register before downloading the file.** Download the file to your python directory and extract the file.

Exercises: We will be applying all we have learned here.

1. Import pandas as pd
2. Import the CSV file into Jupyter notebook, assign it to a variable 'Sal', and display the first 5 values.
   Hint: use the **.head()** *method to display the first 5 values of a data frame. Likewise,* **.tail()** *is used for displaying the last 5 results. To specify more values, pass* **'n=value'** *into the method.*
3. What is the highest pay (including benefits)?   Answer: 567595.43
   Hint: Use data frame column indexing and **.max()** *method.*
4. According to the data, what is 'MONICA FIELDS's Job title, and how much does she make plus benefits?

Answer: Deputy Chief of the Fire Department, and $ 261,366.14.

Hint: *Data frame column selection and conditional selection works (conditional selection can be found under Example 72. Use column index =='string' for the Boolean condition).*

5. Finally, who earns the highest basic salary (minus benefits), and by how much is their salary higher than the average basic salary. Answer: NATHANIEL FORD earns the highest. His salary is higher than the average by $ 492827.1080282971.

Hint: *Use the* **.max()***, and* **.mean()** *methods for the pay gap. Conditional selection with column indexing also works for the employee name with the highest pay.*

Part 3: MACHINE LEARNING WITH PYTHON

Chapter 15. What is machine learning

This technological approach is radically different from the way companies traditionally exploit data. Instead of starting with business logic and applying the data, machine learning techniques allow data to create logic. One of the key benefits of this approach is the removal of commercial assumptions and prejudices that may lead managers to customize a strategy that may not be the best.

The different benefits that come with machine learning, it is time to move on and learn a bit more about some of the other things that you are going to be able to do with this as well. As you start to work with the process of machine learning a bit more, you will find that there are a lot of different ways that you are able to use it and many programmers are taking it to the next level to create things that are unique and quite fun.

Chapter 16. categories of machine learning

The Machine Learning algorithms can fall either in the supervised or unsupervised or reinforced learning.

Supervised Learning

For the case of supervised learning, the human is expected to provide both the inputs and the outputs which are desired and furnish the feedback based on the accuracy of the predictions during training. After completion of the training, the algorithm will have to apply what was applied to the next data.

The concept of supervised learning can be seen to be similar to learning under a teacher's supervision in human beings. The teacher gives some examples to the student, and the student then derives new rules and knowledge from these examples so as to apply this somewhere else.

It is also good for you to know the difference between the regression problems and classification problems. In regression problems, the target is a numeric value, while in classification; the target is a class or a tag. A regression task can help determine the average cost of all houses in London, while a classification task will help determine the types of flowers based on the length of their sepals and petals.

Unsupervised Learning

For the case of unsupervised learning, the algorithms do not expect to be provided with the output data. An approach called deep learning, which is an iterative approach, is used so as to review the data and arrive at new conclusions. This makes them suitable for use in processing tasks which are complex compared to the supervised learning algorithms. This means that the unsupervised learning algorithms learn solely from examples without responses to these. The algorithm finds patterns from the examples on its own.

Supervised learning algorithms work similarly to how humans determine any similarities between two or more objects. Majority of recommender systems you encounter when purchasing items online work based on unsupervised learning algorithms. In this case, the algorithm derives what to suggest to you for purchase from what you have purchased before. The algorithm has to estimate the kind of customers whom you resemble, and a suggestion is drawn from that.

Reinforcement Learning

This type of learning occurs when the algorithm is presented with examples which lack labels, as it is the case with unsupervised learning. However, the example can be accompanied by a positive or a negative feedback depending on the solution which is proposed by the algorithm. It is associated with applications in which the algorithm has to make decisions, and these decisions are associated with a consequence. It is similar to trial and error in human learning.

Errors become useful in learning when they are associated with a penalty such as pain, cost, loss of time etc. In reinforced learning, some actions are more likely to succeed compared to others.

Machine learning processes are similar to those of data mining and predictive modeling. In both cases, searching through the data is required so as to draw patterns then adjust the actions of the program accordingly. A good example of machine learning is the recommender systems. If you purchase an item online, you will get an ad which is related to that item, and that is a good example of machine learning.

Chapter 17. qualitative examples of machine learning applications

In statistical modeling, you might notice that reversion analysis aims to be a process which helps estimate the various relationships between different variables. This will include several techniques that are typically used for variable analysis and matching when several variables are worked with at once whenever you are showing the relationship between independent and dependent variables.

Reversion analysis is a valuable tool when it comes to understanding how the usual value for variable changes over time. Reversion will also help you estimate the conditional expectation of a variable that depends on the independent variable and the average value of said variable. Briefly put, it will shorten the time you spend while juggling multiple values.

More uncommon are situations where you will be presented with a variable that depends on the independent variable along with its quantile or location parameters for the conditional distribution. Usually, the estimate you come to will be an expression for the independent value. We call this the reversion expression. In reversion analysis, you will be showing your interest in the characterization of the variation of the dependent variable in relation to the expression which we can describe as the probability distribution.

One of the possible approaches is taking a conditional analysis. This will take the estimate for the maximum over the average for the dependent variables, which are, again, based on the independent variable that is given. This allows you to determine if the independent variable is necessary or sufficient for the value that the dependent variable holds.

You will use reversion when you are looking to forecast and when it overlaps with machine learning. It will be a good tool for when you are trying the relationships between dependent and independent variables. When dealing with a restricted circumstance, reversion will be used to infer the causal relationship between the variables. You should be cautious, however, as it may give you a false relationship.

There are several different techniques for reversion. Linear reversion and least squares diversion are two of them. Your reversion expression will be defined as finite numbers which don't have a parameter. Nonparametric reversion is a tool that we will be utilizing when we want to permit the reversion expression to be used as a collection of expressions for infinite dimensionality.

Your performance when it comes to revision analysis is going to be a summary of the methods that you practice as processes for data generation and how it ties back into the reversion approach that you applied. The true form of data generation is not always going to be known as reversion analysis and depends on the extent of your assumptions.

The assumptions you provide will need to be testable so you can see if you have provided the machine with enough data.

Machine Learning and Robotics

I believe that we have helped you grow more familiar with what machine learning is. It should not surprise you that it sparked an interest in robotics and has stayed roughly the same for the past several years. But are robots related to machine learning?

Robotics has not developed too much in the past several years. However, these developments are a great foundation for discoveries to come and some even relate to machine learning.

When it comes to robotics, the following five applications apply in machine learning:

1. **Computer vision:** some would say that robot vision and machine vision are more correct as far as terminology goes. For a very long time, engineers and roboticists have been trying to develop a type of camera that will let a robot process the physical world around him as data. Robot vision and machine vision are two terms that go hand in hand. Their creation can be credited to the existence of automated inspection systems and robot guidance. The two have a very small difference and it comes in regards to kinematics in the use of robot vision. It encompasses the calibration of the comment frame and enhances the robot's ability to affect its surroundings physically.

The already impressive advances in computer vision that have been instrumental in coming up with techniques that are geared for prediction learning, has been further helped by a huge influx of data.

2. **Imitation learning:** this is relatively closely connected to observational learning. It is common with kids and has common features, the most obvious being probabilistic models and Batesian. The main question, however, stands. Will it find use in humanoid robots?

Imitation learning has always been an important part of robotics as it has features of mobility that transcend those of factory settings in domains like search and rescue construction, which makes the programming robotic solutions manually a puzzle.

3. **Self-Supervised learning:** Allows robots to generate their training instance due to the self-supervised learning approaches, in order to improve their performance. This includes priority training, as well as data that is captured and is used to translate vague sensor data. The robots with optical devices that have this installed can reject and detect objects.

A solid example called Watch-Bot has been created by Cornell and Stanford. It utilized a laptop and laser pointer, a 3D sensor, and a camera in order to find normal human activities like patterns that are learned through the methods of probability. A laser pointer is used to detect the distance to the object. Humans are notified 60 percent of the time, as the robot has no concept of what he is doing and why he is doing it.

4. **Medical and assistive technologies:** A device that senses and oversees the processing of sensory information before setting an action that is going to benefit a senior or someone with incapacities. This is the basic definition of the assistive robot. They have a capacity for movement therapy, as well as the ability to provide other therapeutic and diagnostic benefits. They are quite cost-prohibitive for hospitals in the US and abroad, so they still haven't left the lab.

Robotics in the field of medicine has advanced at a rapid rate even though they are not used by medical facilities. This advancement can be seen clearly if you see the capabilities of these robots.

5. **Multi-Agent learning:** It offers some key components such as negotiation and coordination. This involves that the robot, based on machine learning, finds equilibrium strategies and adapts to a shifting landscape.

During late 2014, an excellent example of an algorithm used by distributed robots or agents was made in one of MIT's labs for decision and information systems. The robots collaborated and opted to build a more inclusive and better learning model than that which was done by a single robot. They did so via building exploration and teaching them to find the quickest ways through the rooms in order to construct a knowledge base in an autonomous manner.

Chapter 18. python and machine learning

Have you been using the classification as a type of machine learning? Probably yes, even if you did not know about it. Example: The email system has the ability to automatically detect spam. This means that the system will analyze all incoming messages and mark them as spam or non-spam.

Often, you, as an end user, have the option to manually tag messages as spam, to improve the ability to detect spam. This is a form of machine learning where the system takes the examples of two types of messages: spam and so-called ham (the typical term for "non-spam email") and using these cases automatically classify incoming mails fetched.

What is a classification? Using the examples from the same domain of the problem belonging to the different classes of the model train or the "generate rules" which can be applied to (previously unknown) examples.

Dataset Iris is a classic collection of data from the 1930s; This is one of the first examples of modern statistical classifications. These measurements allow us to identify the different types of flower.

Today, the species are identified through DNA, but in the 30s the role of DNA in genetics had not yet been recorded. Four characteristics were selected for each plant sepal length (length of cup slip) sepal width (width of cup slip) petal length, and petal width. There are three classes that identify the plant: Iris setosa, Iris versicolor, and Iris virginica.

Formulation of the problem

This dataset has four characteristics. In addition, each plant species was recorded, as well as the value of class characteristics. The problem we want to solve is: Given these examples, can we anticipate a new type of flower in the field based on measurements?

This is the problem of classification or supervised learning, where based on the selected data, we can "generate rules" that can later be applied to other cases. Examples for readers who do not study botany are: filtering unwanted email, intrusion detection in computer systems and networks, detection of fraud with credit cards, etc.

Data Visualization will present a kind of triangle, circle type, and virginica type of mark x.

The model has already discussed a simple model that achieves 94% accuracy on the entire data set. The data we use to define what would be the threshold was then used to estimate the model.

What I really want to do is to assess the ability of generalization model. In other words, we should measure the performance of the algorithm in cases where classified information, which is not trained, is used.

Transmitting device stringent evaluation and use the "delayed" (Casually, Held-out) data is one way to do this.

However, the accuracy of the test data is lower! While this may surprise an inexperienced person who is engaged in machine learning, it's expected to be lower by veterans. Generally, the accuracy of testing is lower than the accuracy of training. Using the previous examples you should be able to plot a graph of this data. The graph will show the boundary decisions.

Consider what would happen if the decision to limit some of the cases near the border were not there during the training? It is easy to conclude that the boundaries move slightly to the right or left.

NOTES: In this case, the difference between the accuracy of the measured data for training and testing is not great. When using a complex model, it is possible to get 100% accuracy in training and very low accuracy testing! In other words, the accuracy of the training set is a too optimistic assessment of how good your algorithm is. Experiments always measured and reported the accuracy of testing and accuracy on the set of examples that are not being used for the training!

A possible problem with the hold-out validation is that we are only using half of the data used for training. However, if you use too much data for training, assessment error testing is done on a very small number of examples. Ideally, we would use all the data for the training and all the data for testing, but it was impossible.

A good approximation of the impossible ideals is a method called cross-validation. The simplest form of cross-validation is Leave-one-out cross-validation.

When using cross-checking, each example was tested on a model trained without taking into account that data. Therefore, cross-validation is a reliable estimate of the possibilities of generalization model. The main problem with the previous method of validation is a need for training of a large number (the number grows to the size of the set).

Instead, let's look at the so-called v-fold validation. If, for example, using 5-fold cross-validation, the data is divided into five parts, of which in each iteration 4 parts are used for training and one for testing.

The number of parts in the initial set of components depends on the size of the event, the time required for the training model, and so on. When generating fold data, it is very important to be balanced.

Chapter 19. machine learning and data science,

You may also start to notice that there are many different companies, from startups to more established firms, that are working with machine learning because they love what it is able to do to help their business grow. There are so many options when it comes to working with machine learning, but some of the ones that you may use the most often are going to include:

- Statistical research: machine learning is a big part of IT now. You will find that machine learning will help you to go through a lot of complexity when looking through large data patterns. Some of the options that will use statistical research include search engines, credit cards, and filtering spam messages.

- Big data analysis: many companies need to be able to get through a lot of data in a short amount of time. They use this data to recognize how their customers spend money and even to make decisions and predictions about the future. This used to take a long time to have someone sit through and look at the data, but now machine learning can do the process faster and much more efficiently. Options like election campaigns, medical fields, and retail stores have used machine learning for this purpose.

- Finances: some finance companies have also used machine learning. Stock trading online has seen a rise in the use of machine learning to help make efficient and safe decisions and so much more.

As we have mentioned above, these are just three of the ways that you are able to apply the principles of machine learning in order to get the results that you want to aid in your business or even to help you create a brand new program that works the way that you want. As technology begins to progress, even more, you will find that new applications and ideas for how this should work are going to grow as well.

Chapter 20. model validation

Data modeling is an important aspect of Data Science. It is one of the most rewarding processes that receive the most attention among learners of Data Science. However, things aren't the same as they might look because there is so much to it rather than applying a function to a given class of package.

The biggest part of Data Science is assessing a model to make sure that it is strong and reliable. In addition, Data Science modeling is highly associated with building information feature set. It involves different processes which make sure that the data at hand is harnessed in the best way.

Robust Data Model

Robust data models are important in creating the production. First, they must have better performance depending on different metrics. Usually, a single metric can mislead the way a model performs because there are many aspects in the classification problems.

Sensitivity analysis describes another important aspect of Data Science modeling. This is something that is important for testing a model to make sure it is strong. Sensitivity refers to a condition which the output of a model is meant to change considerably if the input changes slightly. This is very undesirable because it must be checked since the robust model is stable.

Lastly, interpretability is an essential aspect even though it is not always possible. This is usually related to how easy one can interpret the results of a model. But most modern models resemble black boxes. This makes it hard for one to interpret them. Besides that, it is better to go for an interpretable model because you might need to defend the output from others.

How Featurization Is Achieved

For a model to work best, it must require information that has a rich set of features. The latter is developed in different ways. Whichever the case, cleaning the data is a must. This calls for fixing issues with the data points, filling missing values where it is possible and in some situations removing noisy elements.

Before the variables are used in a model, you must perform normalization on them. This is achieved using a linear transformation on making sure that the variable values rotate around a given range. Usually, normalization is enough for one to turn variables into features once they are cleaned.

Binning is another process which facilitates featurization. It involves building nominal variables which can further be broken down into different binary features applied in a data model.

Lastly, some reduction methods are important in building a feature set. This involves building a linear combination of features that display the same information in fewer dimensions.

Important Considerations

Besides the basic attributes of Data Science modeling, there are other important things that a Data Scientist must know to create something valuable. Things such as in-depth testing using specialized sampling, sensitivity analysis, and different aspects of the model performance to improve a given performance aspect belong to Data Science modeling.

Chapter 21. machine learning case studies

To help you understand just how deep the field of deep learning goes and just how much it has changed everyone's lives already, I will dedicate this section to showing you specific examples of deep learning and how it is used in its myriad of applications.

Keep in mind, this is not meant to advertise any kind of product or service, but to show you that deep learning is far more common than many people think and that it is not a field pertaining to the higher levels of each industry, but one that belongs to all of us to some extent.

So, without further ado, let's dive in:

Image Curation on Yelp

Although Yelp may not be as popular as it used to be, it still has a very important role to play in how people experience the new places in their living areas (or the different locations they visit as tourists, for example).

At first, Yelp may seem like anything but a tech company - but they are using actual machine learning to make sure their users come back to the site because it provides them with actual, helpful information.

More specifically, Yelp has developed a machine learning system capable of classifying, categorizing, and labeling images submitted by users - but more importantly, this system helps Yelp do this in a genuinely efficient way. This is extremely important for the company, given the huge amounts of image data they receive every day.

Pinterest Content

Who knew searching for wedding ideas on Pinterest is fueled by machine learning?

Pinterest's main purpose is that of curating existing content - so it makes all the sense in the world that they have invested in machine learning to make this process faster and more accurate for their users.

The system developed by Pinterest is capable of moderating spam and helping users find content that is more relevant to their own interests, their styles, and their searches.

Facebook's Chatbots

By this point, it is more than likely that you have stumbled upon at least one chatbot in Facebook Messenger.

These apparently simplistic chatbots are, in fact, a form of primordial artificial intelligence. Sure, Skynet is not typing from the other end of the communication box, but even so, chatbots are a fascinating sub-field of artificial intelligence - one that is developing quite steadily.

Facebook Messenger allows any developer to create and submit their own chatbots. This is incredibly helpful for a variety of companies that emphasize their customer service and retention, because these chatbots can be used for this precise purpose. Sometimes, Messenger chatbots are so well-built that you may not even realize that you are talking to a, "robot."

Aside from chatbots, Facebook invests a lot in developing AI tools capable of reading images to visually impaired people, tools capable of filtering out spam and bad content, and so on.

In some ways, a company that might not seem to have a lot to do with technological innovation is pushing the boundaries of one of the most exciting fields of the tech world: artificial intelligence.

Google's Dreamy Machines

Google is one of the companies constantly investing in artificial intelligence (often, with amazing results). Not only have they developed translation systems based on machine learning, but pretty much every area of their activity is somewhat related to artificial intelligence too.

Don't be fooled - Google has its hands in much more than search engines. In recent years, they have invested a lot in a very wide range of industries, including medical devices, anti-aging tech, and, of course, neural networks.

The DeepMind network is, by far, one of the most impressive neural network research projects ran by Google. This network has been dubbed as the "machine that dreams" when images recreated by it were released to the public, opening everyone's eyes to how artificial intelligence, "perceives" the world.

Baidu Voice Search

Since China is the leading country in artificial intelligence research, it only makes sense that their leading search company, Baidu, is heavily invested in the realm of artificial intelligence too.

One of the most notable examples here is their voice search system which is already capable of mimicking human speech in a way that makes it undistinguishable form, well, **actual** human speech.

IBM's Watson

We couldn't have missed Watson from this list, mostly because this is one of the first impressively successful artificial intelligence endeavors in history.

Most people know IBM's Watson from its participation in **Jeopardy!**, but the supercomputer built by the super tech giant IBM can do **much** more than just compete in televised shows.

In fact, Watson has proved to be very useful to hospitals, helping them propose better treatment in some cancer cases. Given the paramount importance of this type of activity in medicine, it can be said that Watson helps to save actual lives - which is a truly great example of how AI can serve mankind.

Salesforce's Smart CRM

Salesforce is one of the leading tech companies, specifically in the field of sales and marketing, where the tool helps businesses maximize their sales potential and close more deals with their customers.

Salesforce is based on a machine learning tool that can predict leads and assigns scores for each of them. For sales people and marketing pros, this is a true gold mine because it makes the entire sale process smoother, more fluent, and, overall, more efficient.

Where Do You Come From, Where Do You Go, Deep Learning?

Clearly, deep learning advances are quite fascinating. Many take them for granted simply because the speed at which they have developed in recent years means that every year brings a new tool to the market - a tool to use in medicine, healthcare, business, commerce, and more.

The future of deep learning cannot be predicted with certainty - if we had an ultra-powerful AI, it might be able to make an accurate prediction of what will happen next. Even so, **human brains** figure that the following will happen over the next few years:

Better Learning

The more they learn, the more powerful machines become. We have a long way to go before we see the first full AI that is capable of mimicking thought processes and emotions - but the more AI is learning, the faster it will continue to grow.

As I was saying earlier in this book, it is a snowballing effect - so the more the "machine learning ball" is rolling, the larger it will become, and the more strength it will have.

Better Cyber Attack Protection

While humans might be able to beat codes created by humans, it might be a little more difficult for hackers to break in when an AI is protecting the realms of data held by a company. Soon enough, artificial intelligence will be capable of better monitoring, prevention, and responses when it comes to database breaches, DDoS attacks, and other cyberthreats.

Better Generative Models

Generative models aim to mimic human beings as much as they can, in very specific areas. The Baidu example in the previous section is a very good indicator here. Over the next few years, we will start to see a lot more of these very convincing generative models, to the point where we will not be able to make a clear distinction between humans and machines (at least in some respects).

Better Training for Machines

Machine learning training is fairly new, given the rapid ascension of this industry in the past couple of decades. The more we train our machines, however, the better we will become at it - and this means that the machines themselves will be able to make better, more accurate decisions.

Part 4 :
WORKBOOK

So far we've discussed the theoretical and technical aspects of data science and machine learning, but there is one more addition to your skillset that needs to be addressed, and that's visualization. Creating visualizations with Python is vital for any aspiring data scientist because it can easily enrich a project and communicate information a lot more clearly and efficiently.

Visualization involves the use of plots, graphics, tables, interactive charts, and much more. Viewing data through an artistic representation helps users greatly in analyzing it because, let's face it, looking at colorful charts makes things clearer than endless strings of numbers that tire your eyes. Visualization helps with operations that involve data comparisons, complex measurements, or identifying patterns.

The basics of visualization and explore tools such as matplotlib and bokeh. Knowing how to efficiently communicate information to others is a crucial skill, and even though you are only at the beginning of your journey, you should get an idea of the concepts and tools behind visualization.

Matplotlib

Since visualization is a complex topic that requires its own book, we are going to stick to the basics of using Python to create various graphic charts.

So what is matplotlib? It is basically a Python package that is designed for plotting graphics. It was created because there was little to no integration between the programming language and other tools designed specifically for graphical representations. If you already became familiar with MATLAB, you might notice that the syntax is very similar. That's because this package was heavily influenced by MATLAB and the module we are going to focus on is fully compatible with it. The "matplotlib.pyplot" module will be the core of this basic introduction to visualization.

Creating, improving, and enriching your graphical representation is easy with plypot commands, because with this module you can make changes to instantiated figures. Now let's go through some examples and discuss the basic guidelines that will allow you to create your own visualization draft.

First, you need to import all the modules and packages by typing the following lines in Python:

In: import numpy as np

import matplotlib.pyplot as plt

import matplotlib as mpl

Now let's start by first drawing a function. This is the most basic visualization, as it requires only a series of x coordinates that are mapped on the y axis. This is known as a **curve representation** because the results are stored in two vectors. Keep in mind that the precision of the visual representation depends on the number of mapping points

But what if we want to visualize our data by using a histogram? Histograms are one of the best visualization methods when we want to clearly see how variables are distributed. Let's create an example where we have two distributions with standard deviation.

Interactive Visualization

Interactive visualization that is processed inside a browser became very popular due to the success of D3.js, which is a JavaScript library used for creating web-based data visualization with interactive features. This tool is preferred over other methods because there is no latency, meaning data is delivered fast, and visualization can be personalized in many ways.

For Python, we have a similar tool to D3.js called Bokeh (a Japanese term used in photography). This can be found as a component of the pydata stack and is fully interactive, customizable, and efficient. The creation of visual representation methods that are otherwise complex and time consuming for the data scientist. With Bokeh, you can create interactive plots, dashboards, charts, and other visual representations that can handle even large data sets.

For the purposes of this book, we are going to discuss this topic only briefly and focus on matplotlib-based plots. Feel free to explore this tool on your own, because it is intuitively designed with the user in mind and the documentation for it is plentiful.

We create an html file and upload it to the browser. If you used Jupyter until this point, keep in mind that this kind of interactive visualization won't work with it due to our output preference, which is the output_file. Now you can use any website to incorporate the output. Next, you will notice that there are various tools on the right side of the plot. These tools allow you to personalize the chart by enlarging it, and manipulating it with dragging and scrolling. Bokeh is an interactive tool that can be integrated with other packages as well. If you become familiar with tools such as Seaborn or ggplot, you can transfer the visual representation from them into Bokeh. The method used to achieve this is "to_bokeh" and it simply ports charts from other visualization tools. You can also use pandas functions together with Bokeh, such as data conversions.

Quiz

1. When is it Right to Apply Machine Learning?
2. Why is Machine Learning important?

3. Big Data? How does it matter?

4. Why Security Data Science?

5. What is the Reason for Increased Ransom ware Attacks and Data Breaches?

Answers

1. When you are about to work on a complex task or issue, that is the perfect time to apply Machine Learning.

2. An increase in Big Data makes Machine Learning an essential method to solve problems such as:

- Image processing and computer vision

- Energy production for load forecasting

- Computational finance for algorithmic trading and credit scoring

- Natural language processing to help recognize a voice

- Aerospace, automotive, and manufacturing for predictive maintenance

3. Big Data describes data sets that have a size that surpass the normal function of database software tools such as storage, capturing, and analyzing.

It refers to a collection of data sets that are very large and complex such that one cannot process using simple database management tools.

4. This is focused on upgrading information security via practical applications of Statistics, Data Analysis, Machine Learning, and Data Visualization. While the tools and techniques are not different

compared to those applied in Data Science, this field has a major focus on decreasing risk and identification of fraud.

5. There are quite a number of reasons to explain the rise in ransom ware attacks and data breaches:

- Attackers discover an efficient way to generate quick cash using ransom ware. One reason for this is that you can find ransom ware as a service on the dark Web. As a result, attackers can choose to leverage on the ransom ware service and concentrate on the ransom extortion.

- The attack surface has increased, and the network perimeter is dissolved as a result of cloud and mobile.

- Attackers have increased the number of tools as a means to escape the current information security tools.

- The information security team has insufficient cameras to monitor movements of an intruder in the network enterprise. Therefore, adversaries have an advantage because they can move in any direction within the network of an enterprise.

Conclusion

Without any trace of doubt, machine learning and deep learning are two of the most exciting and interesting fields of study at the moment.

There are, truly, a million reasons to love artificial intelligence in general:

1. It is mankind's offspring
2. It brings together multiple disciplines
3. It improves productivity and efficiency
4. It is torn out of a SF movie (and yes, this might actually be a reason for some)

There are a lot of reasons to fear the advent of the AI era as well - starting with the fact that it comes with serious ethical implications and ending with the fact that nobody can tell you just how far AI will go and how, "sentient" it will become.

The book at hand did not aim to be a manual in Python or programming or even deep learning in general - but an incursion into the **realm** of these subjects, a short trip to make you curious about what Python and deep learning are all about, why they are used in association, and even **how** they are used, at times.

I know you will take the information presented here and use it to the best of your abilities, helping yourself create the future you want for your children, nephews, or simply neighbors.

Because, yes, as a data programmer, you belong to the future just as much as robots do. It means that even if everything in the world will be automated, your skills might still be needed. And it's great news from the point of view of the job satisfaction you get as well -

because who doesn't love being useful and creating something as awesome as machines that are capable to save lives, predict financial situations, or simply make entertainment...more entertaining?

My purpose with this entire book was to show you that although deep learning is a truly intricate subject and that there is **a lot** to it, you can still be part of it if you put your mind to it. Python programming is, as I have repeatedly said it throughout the book, one of the easiest types of programming you can learn.

Its intuitive nature and the fact that you don't have to know how to program in more, "elevated" languages make it a truly beginner-friendly programming language even for people who have not written a line of code in their entire lives.

So, if you are interested in the realm of deep learning and the fascinating innovations it brings to the table, if you want a job that is future-proof or if you simply want to take on a challenge you will always remember, Python is for you. Even more, Python for deep learning is for you too, even if you have zero experience in programming.

Hopefully, I managed to instill curiosity in you - by showing you how simple Python can be, by showing you what artificial intelligence is all about, and by showing you clear examples of how AI is used in everyday applications without you even knowing about it.

Maybe even more importantly, I hope I helped you understand that AI and deep learning are not evil (or at least not inherently so), and that there are important ethical issues we should all discuss before it's too late in any way.

There are, of course, many other things that could have been discussed, beginning with the actual intricacies of Python and ending with newly arising ethical issues. What I meant to do is cover the very basics: the things you should absolutely know when you start showing an interest in this amazing field of science.

Because, yes, deep learning is a science by this point. It may have been fiction at the beginning of the 20th century and it may have been seen as delusional towards the middle of the same century but today, in 2019, deep learning is as real as it gets.

Artificial intelligence is, without the slightest trace of doubt, the final frontier in man-made computational sciences. It is the ultimate goal - the one that might help us live longer and happier, the one that might help us find a solution to the fact that we cannot exceed the speed of light, the one to help mankind make decisions based not on emotions and hunches, but on raw data.

Sure, this comes with its downfalls, as it was discussed in the last chapter of this book.

But if you are ready to embrace it all, you are ready to face the future with the largest possible smile on your face.

If you are ready to embrace Python even as a complete beginner, you are a daring soul who deserves to be part of the amazing future we're building in this industry.

If you are ready to embrace deep learning not just as a mere user, but as a programmer lying behind the inner works of these neural networks, you are a true pioneer in the grand scheme of things.

Hopefully, my book here has instilled all these sentiments in you - and it has made you ask all the important questions too.

What's next?

Get down and dirty with Python, learn its basics, and start coding. Just like riding a bike, writing programs for machine learning cannot happen without those first awkward steps - so stay optimistic, erase, try again, erase again, and then try once more.

The future is at your fingertips.

Use it wisely!

Printed in Great
Britain
by Amazon